ALICE'S STORY

as told to

DANA BAGSHAW

Third edition

Table of Contents

Prologue

I see Alice whiz by nearly every day on her bicycle. She lives around the corner from me. I first met her when swimming with the Silver Dolphins at the Boy's Club pool. "My legs aren't good," she said, "so I ride my bike." Now whenever she sees me she jumps down from her bike and says hello. "No, I don't wear a helmet. Old people don't need one." Her bright button of a face appears about a foot lower than mine and I'm five foot two. Through her

1

sparkling eyes you can see her brain working from Chinese to English to form the words, and that she appreciates the challenge.

In the winter, through my window, I still see her whiz by, but I can't catch her. One day I do a double take. I think I see her pass by sitting in one of those electric travel scooters, a flag fluttering behind her, her face so stony I hardly recognized her. Then a few days later whizzing by again on a different, smaller bike.

Finally on New Year's Day, feeling my usual post-holiday let-down, I decide to take my watercolors outside and sit in a warm spot in the sun to paint. I'm putting on the finishing touches on a landscape of our succulents, when here comes Alice heading home on her little bike. She waves to me but keeps going. I call out to her, and walk down the sidewalk to catch up with her.

I ask her point blank what's going on.

"Oh, Otto got me that scooter. He tells me not to ride a bicycle. I'm too old. I'm eighty. But I don't like that scooter. Too slow.

"Otto is my son's name. It's German. His German professor gave him that name."

2

"And who gave you your name of Alice?"

"I did. It's from Beethoven." She starts humming the tune of Fur Elise. *"Only I didn't know how to say it, so it came out Alice."*

And something else I've been wanting to ask her. *"Are you still doing Tai Chi?"*

"Oh, yes. Everyday."

"I just had a bone scan and Tai Chi is recommended."

She doesn't understand.

"Osteoporosis?"

"Ah, osteoporosis," she stumbles through the word. *"That's my disease."*

"May I join you in doing Tai Chi?"

She seems embarrassed but agrees. Have I been too pushy? Am I imposing on her private meditation time?

I join her at the appointed hour on a platform just outside her condo, looking over the lagoon. We face the setting sun. She says some sing-song words in Chinese, then translates: *"the Chinese say: sun sets, day done."* She struggles with transforming the Chinese terms for Tai Chi into English for me. Don't

3

worry, I say, I'll just follow you. But some of her translations are delightful like "reaching for the sky."

We finish with "jumping" -- something she says her master added to the forms. Oh, the knees. So, I don't jump but just bounce a little. Then, trying to acknowledge her as my master, I align my hands in prayer position and bow to her.

She laughs, comes up and hugs me and says, "Please come again. I live alone. I'm lonely."

So my life is enriched by Alice. I join her when I can, and gradually learn her story. We zigzag through her incredible life together.

1. Little Fool

童年

My mom was such a character. A little bit crazy. My father? I don't remember very much of him. A year after the Japanese War began in 1937 with that famous event at the Lugou Bridge, he left us to go with his army. I think my parents were quarrelling before he left because my mom had a bad temper, and once she told me she got a gun and wanted to kill my father. Before I was born she played mahjang, sometimes for three days and three nights she sat at the table, the servants giving her something to eat – playing all the time. Two of her sons died when they were three years old, because my mom would always be playing mahjang, and didn't take care of them. She would leave them to the nanny, and they died.

Then with me, the same as my mom's other children, when I was three – I got very sick. This time my mom stopped playing mahjang and took care of me, because she had lost two children and didn't want to lose me. She had learned her lesson, yes. She started calling me Sagua (little fool), because she believed if she called me that I wouldn't die. So I got to live and she stopped playing mahjang. They still called me Sagua until I was five or six. We lived in the south province of Fujian then and after I got well we moved to Hangzhou, southwest of Shanghai. An American Baptist pastor there said, "You have to believe in God, the Father in the Heavens." The pastor told everyone to believe in God and to stop playing mahjang. My mom started going to his church on Sundays and became very religious.

Alice lives in a small apartment, with an upright piano separating her bedroom from her sitting room with its desk and computer, bookcase, and T.V. Each day when I knock on the door she wants to go outside. We sit at a round, redwood picnic table in a common area for the residents, next to raised beds of gardens the tenants are allowed to tend. To the west we look across a lagoon. I bring along a little dictating device and begin to record the sessions. In this way we progress through her story.

My father served in the army, the Kuomintang. He first married my mother's older sister, my aunt, who was a traditional feudalist. Her feet were bound, very tiny, and she just stayed at home with the children and kept house. She had three children, my older sister and two brothers.

But my mom was different, a very strong character. She fought against feudalism and did whatever the modern girls at that time did. When they tried to bind her feet, she would take off the bindings and throw them away. My father started to notice my mother. He changed his love and she became his second wife.

When my father got his orders to go with the army to the northwest, he took my mom with him, and left the first wife. He put my mom's sister aside because he liked my mom better. It was typical at that time in China for a bureaucrat to have more than one wife. A wife in the city and one in the country, or one that would travel with him. My mother was very brave and travelled with my father. I think she was young, not even twenty, when she first left with my father.

I was my mom's only child, but not my father's. I was born 1932 in the northwest and I travelled with my parents until we settled in Hangzhou – that famous ancient capital of the Song dynasty, and now the capital of Zhejiang province. It's called Heaven on Earth by the Chinese. My father bought my mom a house near a small river. He also bought a girl to look after me. She was maybe five years older than me. They bought the girl for me because they thought since I was the only child I was too lonely and needed someone to play with me. I played with the girl and I loved her very much. We shared a bedroom upstairs. I could hear my parents arguing below.

My mom never hit me, but after my father left, when she would have a temper she would often hit the girl. The girl didn't cry, but I cried and said "STOP, STOP." Once my mother took a duster by the feathers and started hitting at her with the handle. I grabbed my mother around the legs and begged, "Don't hit her." I cried out, "Don't hit, don't hit."

9

One day when we came back from the church, after leaving the girl behind for cooking or doing something, my mom discovered that she had run away and stolen all my mom's treasures: rings, bracelets, necklaces, all jade and gold – all her valuable things gone. My mom was so unhappy, but she was a strong woman and she asked some detectives and they found out that someone had taken the girl to the countryside and it cost my mom a lot of money to get some of the gold and jade back. But the girl never came back. I don't think she herself would steal like that, that someone else who knew the relationship between her and my mom led her to do it. Who, I don't know, just someone who knew our family and knew when we'd be at church. You see, during this time, my mom was the wife of an official of high rank in the army, and they knew she had valuable things. We also had silver money, yuan – round like a nickel, but bigger and very heavy.

Once, after both my father and the girl were gone, my mom showed me a photo of herself on a horse, wearing a cape. She looked about thirty in the photo.

She told me she learned to ride a horse and so she could follow the army with my father, wherever the troops went, and that she liked to travel.

She said she wanted me to understand my background so she would take me to the country to visit my grandma in the country.

I asked my mom why she called me Sagua, little fool. When she explained, I said, "I won't die, so you don't need to call me Sagua anymore."

No, she didn't hold or hug me. That's not the Chinese way. You just look someone in the eye when you talk to them and smile. But when I told her not to call me Sagua anymore, I didn't look her in the eye.

Alice pauses to reflect. "My story is typical," she says, "typical of Chinese from that period." She blinks, looks across the horizon, then adds, "Yes, my story is worthy," looks at me, and begins again.

My grandparents lived in the country northwest of Shanghai, near Changzhou in the Jiangshu province. They were feudal landlords with many rice fields irrigated by canals from the river. They hired local farmers to plant and harvest the rice, and make wine from it. My grandfather had died before I came there. But my grandma had longevity – I think maybe she died around the age of ninety – and she still ran the wine business.

I don't remember much about the trip when my mom took me to see her. I can picture a big house and a small river in front of a small gate. Mostly I remember meeting for the first time my sister, the daughter of my aunt who was my mother's older sister.

Later I look up rice wine-making on the internet. I picture Alice's grandma as she shuffles around on bound feet between racks of steamed rice, telling the local farmers to test the temperature again and again. Apparently they need just the right moment before cooling it down to make the seed-mash starter for the wine. Satisfied at last, her grandma scoops up a serving of the lovely, sweet-smelling mush and gives it to Alice in a little dish. As Alice spoons it in her mouth, she thinks this must be what heaven tastes like. While she carefully tastes each spoonful of the rice mush, her sister-cousin eats hers in no time and asks for more! Alice is amazed by this.

After we got back from visiting my grandma, my mom had enough space in the big house to welcome my brother from the countryside. He was the son of my father's first wife – my mother's older sister. So yes, he was both my brother and my cousin. I felt very happy to have a brother, and life was good.

But in 1940, when I was eight, the Japanese came and occupied our town and our lives changed.

"After Chinese New Year, now comes the full moon," Alice tells me when we finish our Tai Chi, "so we have another festival: the Moon Festival. I will make little rice balls for the holiday, and I will bring you some this week-end."

The weekend comes and goes. No rice balls, no Alice. On Monday I go over to see her and she says, "Oh, I'm sorry. So many people came to see me. They ate all the rice balls!"

2. Japanese Occupation

日寇统治

The Japanese did everything terrible, cruel – hit, capture the women and yes, rape the women. Not only the Japanese did bad things, but the Chinese police, hanjin we called them, spies. A young man like my brother would be captured and told, "You are a Chinese soldier. You are the enemy. We will shoot you." So my brother ran away.

My mother and I hid under the floor in our house in a spot covered by two lose boards. We lived underground all the time. We kept our food there and slept on blankets on the earth. The Japanese could come find us any time, but one day a Japanese soldier did come. He opened the boards and looked in for a long time, but then he left. We were afraid he would bring more men back, so we got up and ran to find some place else to hide. We only got as far as the street outside the gate near the river when we saw

Japanese soldiers, a lot of them, and no way to escape, so my mom grabbed me and we jumped into the river. It was winter and the water was very cold. She swam down the river with me to another spot where some people saved us and took us to the Baptist church's refuge.

Because they took us in at the refuge, we became Christian. But we worried about my brother. Once my mom carried me outside the dormitory into the yard. It was snowing – the ground was covered with snow. We knelt there in the snow and prayed that my brother would come back. "Please, God, save him." And he did! One day my brother came back and told us how the Japanese had captured him. They tied him up and added him to a long line of other men, and aimed their guns at them to shoot, but the Japanese got an order "Leave as soon as possible," so they took their weapons and went away, but left the men alive, still tied up together. "That's God's will," my mom said. And the pastor said God saved my brother. And since then my mom became a faithful Christian and she really, REALLY, believed in God.

In the Baptist refuge, I started primary school. My mom helped with the teaching. While we were there we didn't know what was happening to our house. But after the attack on Pearl Harbor in 1942, the Japanese withdrew from our town and left a Chinese puppet government to carry out their policies, so we were able to go back home. We found nothing inside but the ceiling and the floor. No rooms. They must have taken our storage boxes made of camphor and burned them on the floor to keep warm. They had turned our house into a place for horses, yes, a stable. Everything was gone. My mom put boards back in for walls and we lived very simply again in the big house.

My mom began teaching at the municipal primary school. I think maybe my papa had paid for her teacher's training before the war. So I went to school with her and was in a different class. But after a year I went back to the Baptist school and my mom, I think, stopped teaching, at least full-time.

My mom taught me how to ride her bicycle. It was unusual for a woman or a girl to ride a bike, so people stared at me in amazement when I rode past

16

them on my way to school. "Oh such a girl. Riding a bicycle. What a wonder!"

She also taught me how to swim at a small lake nearby. She wore a wool swimsuit the color of the sky, and when I was a teenager I wore her blue swimsuit.

I notice a red rash around Alice's eyes and interrupt her to ask if the sun is bothering her. Maybe she should wear sunglasses.

"Maybe, it's because of my dream."

"Your dream?"

"Last night I dreamed I was walking along a dark path with some other people. They were behind me. Then I got to a big open space, but I was alone. No one was there with me."

It seems she was more afraid of being alone in the open space, than being along the dark path with the others. I'm touched she told me about the dream, but can't see how it could be related to the rash on her eyes, so I don't know what to say.

"Would you like to wear my sunglasses? You're facing right into the sun."

"No, I'm okay, I'm okay." She's thought of something she wants to tell me, and continues her story.

During this time of Japanese occupation, on and off for many years, whenever my mom and I needed to earn money, we carried tea leaves, our hometown's product, over our shoulders – a sack in the front and one in the back, tied together. I carried 15 kg. divided between two sacks and my mom carried more. We had to carry these on the train for five or six hours to Shanghai, report to someone at the market, and bring back things like toothbrushes, toothpaste, towels, socks, clothes, or industrial things, for the shops back in our town. They would pay us when we returned with the goods.

When we got to the train station in Shanghai, and got off in a big yard, there'd be a great crowd of people. Lots of people, carriers like us. The Japanese soldiers, and the Chinese police that worked for them, would order us around telling us, go this way, that way. Depending on the temper or attitude of the men,

18

sometimes they'd just tell us where to go. But often they would be terrible, yell at us, and hit us with their belts, whip us. Sometimes people would fall backwards, get caught underfoot and be trampled. We would give money to the policemen so they would let us go. But sometimes they didn't want our money. They would just hit. We never knew what might happen.

If they didn't take our money, we would buy extra items and bring them back for our neighbor to sell from her house. Usually I went with mom on the weekends, but sometimes, when my mom wasn't teaching and I was in school, she went by herself. I often came home to the big empty house. Our neighbor would look after me if I needed her. Once when I was alone, it began to thunder, so loud. I was the only one there, so small, and so afraid, so I went to my neighbor and it seemed like she saved me.

One time, during Chinese New Year, my mom came home all beat-up with a terrible bruise on her eye, and came back with nothing. And we had only

19

one dish for New Year's dinner – soy bean sprouts and salted cabbage. That's our "fortunate dish" she said. In fact, she was supposed to pay the shop if she came back with no goods, but she didn't pay. We couldn't pay. She just went to another shop the next time.

In 1945 the Americans dropped the atom bomb in Japan. I was in senior middle school. My sister, who first didn't want to leave the countryside, came to live with us, so that made four of us. My brother got a job at the Post Office.

All this time I never saw my father, and I hated him. After he left us, he didn't care about us, no information from him, no economic help. He never sent us letters, never sent us money. I didn't want to even know him. I hated him.

When I was about thirteen, he came back to Shanghai. He wrote my older sister and brother to tell them to come visit him and they said I should go with them for a few days. I wondered what my father looked like, so I went. He was staying in a grand hotel with his third wife and two children. We stayed in another room. He was rich, so renting another room was no problem for him. Once a day we ate in the dining hall in the hotel. He seemed like a stranger to me. The new mom, the sister and brother, were very strange and I wasn't interested in knowing them. I didn't talk to him or to them. At that time, I just didn't care. I hated all of them. I said to myself I don't want to be here, I don't want to be here. I just wanted to go home. When we left my father asked me to write to him, but I never wrote anything. He went to Beijing to get a new job. We remained strangers.

The next time I go to see Alice, her door is closed, but her swimsuit is hanging and dripping on the front porch, so I ring the bell and her caretaker answers. "I'm just beginning to give her a massage," he says.

She is lying down on her bed behind a screen. I hear a rustling of sheets, and she is up greeting me. Stuck to her eyes are slices of cucumber. The rash I saw before has grown much worse.

"My eyes . . . " she begins. When she blinks, the cucumber slices flap at me.

21

"I don't think it was that dream you told me about," I say.

"I think it's something she ate," her caretaker says.

"It could be a reaction to the chlorine in the swimming pool," I say. *"I used to get that when I went swimming."*

I hand her an offering.

"Oh. Oranges from your tree!" she cries with appreciation.

I nod and say I'll come back another time. I try to hug her but this time she doesn't want that, pointing to her eyes. I go home and do Tai Chi on my own, but it's not the same.

Two days later I call on Alice again. She greets me at her door wearing sunglasses. Her eyes are much better. No, she didn't go swimming, she played ping-pong instead at the community center.

We go out to our spot for another recording session. She throws her short legs over the side armrest of the redwood chair looking so casual and cool, as if to say: okay lay it on me, what do you want to know? I clear up a few points from the last session and then she begins again.

3. Communist Youth

中学时代

My older brother, twelve years older than me, lived most of the time with my father. When he finished his university education, he came to Hangzhou and lived with me, our mom, and our other brother and sister. I was in middle school. He taught me math and geometry. When I couldn't solve the problems he would help me. All four of us lived in harmony. They loved me and I liked them. I was so happy after being an only child to be living with them.

When I was in senior middle school, I became greatly influenced by one of my senior middle school teachers, who turned out to be an underground Communist. No one knew. She took care of our class and taught us English and Chinese. She was young, maybe only ten years older than me. In our composition class she taught us Communist ideals, and we listened to her with great attention -- I liked listening to her very much. She painted a picture of an ideal society with no exploitation of one class by another. I dreamed about that society and I loved that teacher very much. She introduced to us Soviet novels, "October" and "Iron Current" translated into Chinese, which I took home to read, and they showed me that Communism was better and I believed in it. We also read the so-called autobiography of Pavel Korchagin by Ostrovksky. He was our example, our model and we believed in him. Such books made a deep impression on me. I would ride my bike to the beautiful West Lake in Hangzhou and sit among the bamboo or willow trees and read my Soviet novels and dream about the day when all people would be equal.

I walk home from Alice's feeling thrilled that she is sharing her story with me. I know I'm on to a "worthy" story, just as she said. I've read many novels set in China, but I'd never heard an actual person's story from China. I've also read a few

24

Russian novels, but the idea of Soviet novels being translated and read in China is a new concept to me.

I go straight to my computer and start googleing. Sure enough, Ostrovksky's novel has sold over 10 million copies in China and is still popular there among youth. As recently as the year 2000, the Chinese adapted the novel in a TV series with Ukrainian actors.

I start getting excited about the book Alice and I are building.

I come back the very next day. Alice is wearing a baseball cap with Spanish words on it. "My eyes are much better. Today I take the last pill from the doctor. He gave me a piece of paper that described my disease, but I didn't read much of it."

"That's common practice now in California," I tell her. "They give me those printouts too. Saves them time explaining."

We are both tired from the last session, and I think she must be on antihistamines because she seems more listless, but we've become very determined. We work until sunset, don't even do our Tai Chi, and I learn much more about her past.

25

In 1949 the Communists took power and called the new regime "The People's Republic of China." The Koumintang ran away to Taiwan, and before Communist troops came to my town of Hangzhou, for three or four days, we had no government, and no teachers at our school. It seemed everything had stopped. So we advanced students, three to five of us, a small team, took charge, thinking we had to protect our school. We also went around the city to keep everything safe. We thought we were very important.

When the liberation army finally came into our town, we went to welcome them. We brought them tea, buns, and offered to do whatever we could. It was in May of my second year of my senior middle school and we had two months until summer. I was chosen to attend a Communist course for youth workers for two months that summer and was accepted as a member of the New Chinese Youth League, the preparatory step for becoming a Communist Party member. We were trained as the workers for the party. We were supposed to reform the countryside, go to the landlords to force them to give up their land, their money, and their oxen to the local farmers. But I didn't have to do that. I was assigned to go back to my school. Because it was a Baptist mission school, it was difficult for the Communist Party to deal with it, so they wanted me to be the spokesperson. They "elected" me as president of the student union, but I had to do whatever my political director told me. American teachers were still there, and we had a Chinese principal.

I was not a good Christian. I told our principal that she had to cancel the morning prayers and stop all religious activity in the school. And I had to check her accounts to see if she was putting money into her own pocket. I feel very bad about it now, but I didn't find anything wrong. She was a very dedicated woman, and very clever. She had raised a lot of money through donations. I'm so sorry to know they put her into prison for almost all the rest of her life, for two or three decades. Only after the proletarian Cultural Revolution she got free, and her students, my classmates went to visit her in 1991. And they told her sorry from me because I was in the USA by that time. She died when she was over a hundred years old.

Whenever Alice gets excited or emotional, she isn't so careful with her English.

That last year in my middle school, I never went to class to listen to the teachers. I wasn't a student but a worker – here's a meeting, there's a meeting, I have to go visit someone else! I became active in street propaganda. At the time they had issued paper money, but it seemed not dependable, and the price kept going up, so people were using the paper money to buy the old silver yuan. I went on a truck with a megaphone and yelled out: "Stop buying silver money. It bothers our currency." Other members of the Student League came with me, and we had a volunteer driver. We stopped in the center of town and started playing music, and singing songs to attract more people, and then I went up and continued yelling out the propaganda over a microphone.

Eventually, they closed down the Baptist middle school, and that building became a hospital for women giving birth. Of course the Communists also closed down the Baptist church, and my mother and her Christian friends had to meet in their homes for worship, Bible study, and prayer. Yes, it became an underground church.

Many classmates who had been underground Communists before Liberation, became active, but because they were "intellectuals" most of them did not have good results. I learned later that one killed herself, and the other went mad and was put in a hospital until the end of life.

4. The Russian Institute

俄专

When I arrive in the afternoon, Alice is carrying on a lively conversation over the phone. She hangs up and tells me it's her son, Otto. Across her computer screen march Chinese characters. "I'm reading the news," she explains. But she shuts it down and makes us some green tea. We carry our cups outside to the common area and sit at the table for our story session.

In 1950, the next year of liberation, the party collected students from the whole nation who had completed twelve years of schooling to take a university entrance examination. Even though I never attended classes that last year, I got very high marks. I had always loved trains, and I wanted to be a railway manager. On my application I wrote I wanted to attend the railway department of a university in the liberated area of China, Dalian city. The University was under the control of the Communists when I got there in 1950. I found out that the original Dalian University with lots of departments had been changed to three institutes: industrial, medical, and Russian. They assigned me to the Russian Institute, to learn the language for our new times. I was among the first students of the so-called New China, under the leadership of Mao Zedong. The Chinese ran the institute, but there were a lot of Russian professors.

Up until that time an institute was considered lower than a university. Some students who had old thinking decided to leave, and the authorities shamed them as an example to "educate" us – actually, to scare us: Don't go away. If you leave the institute it will ruin your future. What these students did will always be in their file.

That should have been a warning for me, but I was still happy to be there. The Communist Party had paid for my long trip to the institute. When I went away, my mom gave me money to buy things, but when I got to the institute I wrote her and said, "You needn't send me any money any more. The party gives me everything I need." They gave me a monthly allowance, my room, my food and my clothes: my uniform, my shoes, hat, everything in the army! When I put on my uniform I felt very proud. It looked like the Soviet army's uniform but without any bars on the shoulder.

Yes, the Soviet army was in charge at this point and the Chinese army was still not that public, a little secret.

What was our women's uniform like? Like our male classmates, trousers, but instead of the high collar on the jacket, our collars were turned down.

I lived in a dormitory where I shared a room with six or seven girls. No one else from my town was there, no one I knew. So I had to make all new friends. I made good friends.

Because I was such a fan of Communism, they assigned me to be the head of my whole class. We had more than fifty people in our class, and my job was to organize the class meetings, where we often broke into small groups to talk about some political theme.

When we weren't busy with our studies or party meetings, we liked to get together and sing. During holiday weekends when the office was empty, we would go there and sing from a songbook, turning page after page, learning every song. We learned so fast. The songs were Soviet Union songs, some from movies, folk songs, current popular songs, all bi-lingual in Russian and Chinese. I still have that songbook. The notation is not like Western notes, but follows a numbering system. I had a very small pitch pipe, the size and shape of the cap of an ink pen. I would blow on it to get the starting tone, then we'd follow the numbers and the rhythm.

A sample sheet of music showing the first half of a song:

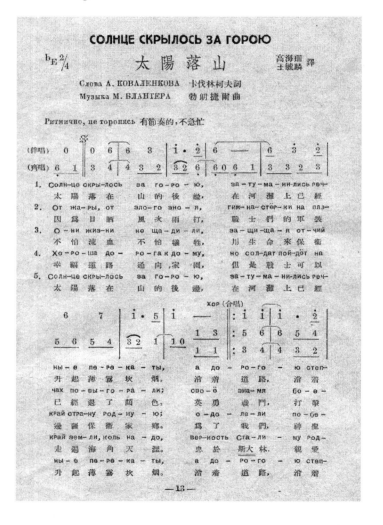

On the weekends we would often go to the dining hall for dancing. In the hot weather, we'd wear short skirts, just over the knee, but usually we'd wear them mid-calf, and sometimes a long skirt. Especially if we had a guest, we would dress up in something special. I liked the waltz, three steps, and the foxtrot, four steps. I couldn't do these dances today. Sometimes we put on performances of folk dances wearing our local traditional costumes.

You see, in China there are sixty different minorities, like from Tibet. My "minority" was Han, but yes, Han was certainly not a minority, and most of us were Han. Mostly the party chose students using their own criteria so not many minority students from the small villages were chosen.

Since the institute was run by the military, everything was first class. They had a nice swimming pool. My mom let me take her blue wool swimsuit with me, and I got to swim in the pool there as well as in the sea – both were cold!

I am so engrossed with the Russian Institute that I forget about the cup of tea Alice has made for me and when I take a sip it's gone cold.

"Oh, so sorry. Next time I'll make butter tea. Butter in the tea makes it stay warmer."

"That's okay. Tell me, Alice, did you have a boyfriend when you went to the institute?"

She squirms a little before answering.

I had a friend in my hometown, but it was nothing, and after I went to the institute we didn't stay in touch. My first year at the institute you might say I had my first "boyfriend". We would meet the boys in the dining hall. I was twenty years old, and a guy in a class three years higher than mine became attracted to me. That guy was always looking for me and brought me to a cinema, and a restaurant, but I didn't feel anything serious. We would make an appointment to meet at the gate of the institute. We were both from Shanghai. He gave me a gold watch. He came from a rich family, capitalists. I didn't object to that, but I didn't feel a deep love. It was just nice to have someone to keep me company. I think at that time I

36

was too young and didn't understand what being in love meant. I just liked the attention and feeling grown up. But he was assigned to another place, and someone told me he got another girlfriend. So I stopped writing to him and I took the gold watch back to his family. It felt right.

At the end of our story session, we begin Tai Chi again, and both of us notice that I am doing the exercises better. I feel like her shadow, following the moves, and fall more easily into her rhythm.

5. Self-Criticism

思想改造

In the first three years at the institute, I still believed in Communism. Although we were very active and wanted to be Communist Party members, the party did not like intellectuals and started one campaign after another against us. They said you must re-build your brain, so you have to make a self-examination. They said: Open your heart to the party. What's in the bottom of your heart, take it out. Be honest to your party. So for three years I wrote about myself and criticized my family. I said my father was a high-ranking officer in the Kuomintang army and an enemy of the people. (Later, I got to know that he helped the liberation army occupy Beijing. He wasn't in the army after the victory over Japan but I didn't know that.) I said I hate him. I wrote this because the party secretary had us draw a line, and say which side is bourgeois and which is proletariat. And I wanted to be in the proletariat front and not in my father's so I had to criticize him. I had to hate him, but actually I really did hate him.

I also wrote about my uncle who was an official of high rank in Kuomintang. And after so-called liberation he went to live with our family, mom and me. He was the husband of my father's sister. Someone told him his life was in danger and he had to leave. Later I learned, he was an enemy of the Communist Party and they say he killed a lot of Communists in the Civil War, the war between Kuomintang and Communists.

I had a family friend, who came back from the USA to be a professor of chemistry at the Dalian Institute. Because he was a neighbor in Hangzhou, and both of us were there at the institute away from our town, during holidays I would go to his home to see him with his wife and two children. He was a member of the Democratic Party, the Nine-three Association of Scholars. We talked a lot about the political campaign in our institute. Later in the mid-fifties he got criticized as one of the right wing and lost his job at the institute, and I didn't even get to say good-bye to him. He was one of the first advanced intellectuals who had their career lives killed by the Communists. Their fate was to go and do labor in the fields.

So because of my connection to him, later when I also got criticized, they said that I was trying to organize right-wing Democrats in the army. But that was not true, just gossip!

I also wrote something about religion and church and how I had been baptised, but I said I had been under the influence of my mom, and I told about how my teacher had changed my mind. I no longer believed in God because I believed in communism. No God. Everything will be done by people. Mao Zedong said "People will get victory over God."

In 1953 when I began teaching new students at the institute and my mom came to see me. She wanted to go to church and she didn't know the way, so I went together with her while I was still in uniform. While she went to the front of the church to worship, I sat on the last row and read a novel. By that time I was reading classic Russian novels: Gogol. Dostoyevsky's

Crime and Punishment. Tolstoy's War and Peace. His fantastic Anna Karenia made a deep impression on me. I read all six of Turgenev's famous novels. I liked Chekhov's sarcasm.

It didn't matter that I didn't believe in God. Somebody reported seeing me at the church, and so I was criticised at a meeting for going to church wearing my uniform and later I was not given a promotion that everyone else got.

During 1955 the first political campaign against us broke out. One of my classmates, Qing, with whom I had a close friendship, became a target of criticism. He was such a talent. He wrote poems and articles. The party said he had fallen politically behind and his brain was full of capitalist ideas. The theme of his poems, they said, was that he didn't know his goal or where he was going, so someone gave him a light, a torch, and he was so thankful that then he could see the future and where to go. His poems were counter-revolutionary, they said, because only the party should be the light. No one should talk to him. He was very lonely. But we were forbidden to talk to him.

I didn't get to read Qing's poems myself. I only knew him for a short time just before that, when the two of us were sent to Beijing to work on a textbook. At that time there was a committee for making our own textbook. My responsibility was for the section on reading articles, and his was for the section on grammar. So we were sent to check any printing mistakes before it was published to make sure everything was completely right, even every period and comma. We had to check it three times. I still keep that textbook we edited together.

I can't remember where we stayed in Beijing, but we didn't stay together. However, we had more time to be together and get to know each other, and we started to become very close. In the evening, we walked to the park, held hands, embraced and kissed. We felt free in the city because we were strangers there. No one knew us in Beijing.

When we got back to the institute, they had started the campaign of criticism. They shut down the classroom teaching. We were all co-workers before we went to Beijing, and when we got back they separated us into two groups in the empty classrooms, to criticize the two most outstanding students in our department. One was Mr. Chen and the other was Qing. I was put in the group to criticize Mr. Chen and I was not allowed to have any contact with Qing. Both men were under guard and watched all the time.

No one dared to talk to Mr. Chen, but a close friend of mine was very brave and loyal to him. She married him. She had been my best friend since 1950 in the dormitory. She was so clever, much more clever than me, I think. She learned Pushkin's famous poem by heart and could recite it from the very beginning to the end. They moved to a room and put their beds together, and that was their marriage. They had no ceremony, no celebration. They were ostracized. My friend was very brave.

But my love of Qing was new. I didn't dare speak to him and he had a cruel fate. He ended up jumping from a very high building. That had a deep effect on me. No one did anything about it when he jumped. I felt so sad, but I could not express it, only keep it within myself. I could talk to no one. Otherwise, they would say I have sympathy with the enemy.

So I loved Qing for only a very short time. I felt a romance was just started when he jumped off the building. Even though I was twenty-four, I wasn't what we Chinese say "ripe" enough. I was naïve, and didn't understand much of life. I didn't know what I was doing.

With Qing's death I lost faith in the Communist Party. I still believed in the Communist ideals, but I became very disappointed with the party. I continued with the self-criticism but I was no longer active with the party. I thought they didn't do things in the right way. They didn't even keep the constitution, just put it aside. I thought if the Communists work in this way, I won't be a member of the party. Like Qing's poem, I had lost my way, didn't know which way to go. For two years I went from active to passive.

6. Marriage & Campaign Against the Right Wing

结婚 一 反右斗争

All this time, I suffered in silence. I could talk to no one. Finally, I found someone I trusted enough to talk to – the first and only person I could talk to. We had both been at the institute since 1950 and we knew a lot about each other. In fact we discovered we had been on the same train, me from Hangzhou and he from Shanghai going to the institute in 1950. He was secretary of the Youth League, so I knew him, but we were not close. We didn't get to know each other because we were studying and teaching in different classes until we were graduate students. Actually, he started teaching half a year earlier than me.

He was such a kind person. Usually, men like him, who were not top leaders, but in the middle, were always trying to advance themselves. They don't care about the masses under them. It's very difficult to be the one in the middle. No one likes them. But my husband was something special. Leaders liked him, and the masses liked him too. He didn't try to climb the ladder. He just did his job, what he was asked to do. They respected him because he was so dedicated to his job. He spoke well and dealt with everyone using patience. He didn't say bad things about anyone. No gossip. Sometimes he knows your shortcomings, but he will just talk to you and no one else. So you could trust him. I felt I could trust him and tell him things I never told anyone.

Alice's husband on the right, with his comrades "at the end of the hardest time of his life," *Alice says.* "They look old here, but they were still young."

In 1955 my husband and I were chosen to go into the advanced graduate class to be re-educated and made into professors – teachers of Russian for the higher grades at the institute. Why was this? Because at that time, relations between the Soviet Union and China were getting worse and worse. The Soviet teachers were leaving, so they needed us, and we were being educated to take over their posts.

Then in 1956 a new campaign started. They said: Tell us every shortcoming of the Communist Party. In this way you can help our party to make some progress. I thought that was good. With an open heart, I said everything I didn't like, everything I had been thinking. I couldn't lie. I was too naïve. I just believed what they said. But it was a trick. What I wrote was added to my list of crimes. Mao Zedong himself later said: "We coaxed the snakes out of the hole and then chopped off their heads." You see, in ancient times the Emporer Ching put seventy-eight scholars in a hole and killed them. But Chairman Mao killed a

hundred times more in his clever, sneaky way –
killing the future of the intellectuals that survived.

We're meeting inside Alice's apartment because there's a chilly wind outside. I ask her if she has a photo of her husband. She shows me a notebook she put together for her granddaughter. Opening it reveals a photo taken shortly after her marriage.

"Look," she points to some Chinese characters, "I've written: On the eve of my bad fortune. You see, the campaign against me began shortly after that." And above the wedding photo, a colorful shot of the two of them many years later, sitting amid a floral exhibition. "Here I wrote: At the Dawn of our Good Fortune," she tells me. "You see, it was after we returned from our stay in California with our hard-earned "US dollars".

In the notebook she also shows me a copy of her favorite song, "Auf Flugeln des Gesange" by Mendelsohn. A song about heaven by the Ganges River in India. She sings it to me in both English and Chinese with perfect timing, making sure she counts through the long sustained note at the end of the last phrase. There's also a poem she wrote in English called "The Hummingbird, because my granddaughter is tiny, like me." And pages and pages of Chinese, hand-written on blue-lined notebook paper. "My granddaughter doesn't read Chinese, but I am trying to motivate her. She says now she wants to learn. She is twenty-six years old. She has a boyfriend, but I don't think she wants to marry. And I put money here in this pocket." Alice pulls out some Chinese money. "Look, she spent all the US dollars, but left the Chinese money."

I look again at the wedding photo. Alice looks so sweet, fresh, and pretty, and her husband looks intelligent and kind. I fall in love with both of them. And I get her to talk more about the time of their "courtship," a word I have to explain to her.

We first started talking in the classroom. We understood each other. We had the same ideas about things. We started to enjoy each other's company. We went to movies. Played ping-pong. But I was seldom thinking of marriage, because the future did not look bright. Still we became very close. We could never hold each other in public like I see young couples do here in America. But in the evening, we went to a seaside park, and there we would sit in the sand or on a bench and hold each other and kiss. One evening he asked me if I would love him. I did love him, but I didn't believe in a future, so I said, "Ya, I love you. What else is there to do?"

On June 1, 1956 we registered for marriage. We moved into a different section of the dormitory, and put our beds together. We had no ceremony, but we did have a celebration – at one of the weekend parties. My friend, who I hadn't talked to since she married

Mr. Chen, came to the party. Her husband didn't dare come, but she came and congratulated me.

So we lived together in one bedroom. In the corridor we shared a toilet, a sink, and a two-burner cooker with two other couples.

We were still in training to take the place of the Soviet professors. But it never happened. A new political campaign had begun and this time I was a target. All I had written in the self-criticism became my crimes.

Was this the Cultural Revolution, I wondered? No, she informs me, that didn't come until ten years later.

My criticism began right after graduation from the Institute. My husband and I wanted to go to Shanghai so we could meet each other's parents, but no, we couldn't go. The new struggle focuses on the members of the so-called right wing. First they announced two weeks for learning the new political policies, and after that they said: "No summer vacation. There is sharp struggle between proletariat and bourgeois class." We had to stay for meeting after meeting and they criticized me again and again for two months. For the whole summer vacation.

They wrote my name and my crimes on big sheets of paper and posted them on the corridor walls of the institute. This was their treatment: just announce in public that the members of the right wing are enemies of the people. Publicly shame them. No one could talk to me. I was glad that no students were there because of the summer vacation. But all the workers saw the writings on the wall, my co-workers, teachers, about sixty of them, our assistants and administrators. My crimes went into my file to follow me the rest of my life. In China, they still do to this day – everyone has a file that goes with you wherever you go. Oh, the file is never in your own hands, you never get to see it. They just say when you apply for a job that they have to check your file, then say you can't have a job. At least I knew my crimes because they had been posted on the walls at the institute. Some people never knew what went into their files.

Mr. Chen and his wife, my girlfriend, were so disappointed from the campaign of 1955 that they left the army and went back to Shanghai.

In 1959 my husband and I had the choice to go back home to Shanghai too, but he didn't want to go because he felt if he left the army he would have too much shame to see his father. And by this time I was pregnant, and my husband thought they would send me to a farm as a laborer. So we stayed longer at the institute, and they assigned me to be a carpenter. I could hammer in a nail, and pull out the nails, paint furniture, put everything in boxes for shipping. And though I'm proud I can still do those things today, at the time I never thought about whether I liked it or not. I just did what I had to do, yes, just accepted my punishment and my isolation.

My husband was still going through the criticism, meeting after meeting, political education, studying and reading important articles in the newspapers. He was still in the army, and had the rank of captain, two stars on his uniform.

After a few months, the institute shut down because relations between the Chinese and the Russians had broken down. They said the institute had finished its historical task and no new students would be accepted. They did, in fact, send most teachers into the fields as workers. That was Mao Zedong's policy. If you are intelligent, so what? You cannot do reading all the time. You must learn about working as a laborer. The 1957 political campaign, was only against intelligent people. The most outstanding were killed or put in prison.

I ask Alice what her husband's name is and she tells me, but says she doesn't want me to use it in the book. "I don't worry about me. I'm an old woman. What can they do to me? But I worry about my daughter and sons who are still in China. The political situation is so changeable there. You never know when it might cause them trouble."

7. Stuck in Hangzhou & Shanghai

四年生活在沪杭

In April 1959, my husband was sent to the Chinese "Siberia" up north, the Province of Heilonjian near the Amur River, northeast of Manchuria. My husband never got exposed in public like I did, never got a political hat, so no one knew what kind of person he was. He had no Kuomintang or right wing connections in his family. Only later in "Siberia" did he find out what they wrote in his file. He had a classmate who became a member of the Gang of Four, so we suspected that man had something to do with it.

When Alice uses the term "political hat" she puts her hands on top of her head. I remember reading once about Chinese people literally being humiliated by being forced to wear a hat bearing Chinese inscriptions, but she says, no, that was later during the "so-called" Cultural Revolution. It seems that a political hat is a figurative way of speaking that means a label or official classification that goes in their records.

Also she consistently uses the term "Siberia" to describe where she was living, though it was south of Russian Siberia.

When first sent to "Siberia," my husband lived in a tent and worked as a laborer, digging a canal for irrigating fields. It is so difficult there because the earth is always frozen. One swing of the pick makes only a tiny hole.

I wasn't sent because of my pregnancy, but after he left I regretted so very much that I didn't go with him, or that I didn't hold on to him and not let him go. Once he left, I had no one to talk to at the institute. I felt so terrible not knowing anything about the future, but after a few weeks or maybe a month, the political co-ordinator told me I could go home to Shanghai to give birth. They gave me ten months salary, which they had cut in half after my criticism. Still it made quite a bulge in my wallet.

While my self-criticism was about the right wing, the campaign had continued against waste, luxury, and holding on to unnecessary material goods. Riding the train back home, I sat by a classmate who was very rich – his girlfriend wore luxurious clothes and they rode in first class quarters on the ship. We sat together all the way to Shanghai and we talked a little, and shared a newspaper. When he went to the dining car he asked me if I would watch his belongings, and when I went to the dining car he said he'd watch mine.

Three days after I arrived in Shanghai, I decided to take my money to the bank. When I got to the counter and opened my purse my money was gone! It had been replaced with little rectangles the same size as the money, cut from that newspaper we'd shared!

I went to the police and an analyst there listened to my story, then he told me how to get it back. Following his instructions, I went to the man's house, knocked on the door and said, "I know you stole my money. Either you give it back to me or I will report you to the police." He said, "Give me three days to think about it." When I went back after the three, he had only one piece of paper to give me. He had written a check that he said I could take to the bank. So I took it, and just hoped it would work. It did. I got my money back.

When it came time for the baby, I went to the hospital and had my first child, my daughter. My husband didn't get to see her until a year later, when he could come down for his winter vacation. That's when I got pregnant with my second child, a son, now known as Otto.

At this point Alice gets a little spark in her eyes. "You see, at that time, we didn't know how to control!"

I laugh with her at the double meaning of her statement.

It's moments like this that I treasure.

Alice continues her story:

For four years from 1958 to 1962, I was sitting there in Shanghai and Hangzhou doing nothing but taking care of my children. No school or institute would accept me. Even after my political hat was removed, and I was no longer classified as a member of the political right, still no one would give me a job.

During that time I translated a Soviet novel. My manuscript grew to a stack of papers about 15" thick. My neighbors' children were students and they liked to read what I translated. They kept waiting and asking me for more. They were very attracted to this story about a Soviet spy in Germany. I've forgotten the author, not one of the famous ones. But the story was gripping – full of suspense and dangerous work. You could not give up on it. The title of the book in Russian meant "Even one in the fighting field is a soldier."

Meanwhile, after two years of being a laborer, my husband became an interpreter for the county leader whenever they went to the other side of the river into Russia. This didn't last long because the relations with Russia were not good. So he got assigned to teach in the middle school.

So after four years of my just sitting in Hangzhou, my husband's county leader, the Communist secretary, said "Let her come here, we need teachers here." When my husband came down for his third visit he told me about it.

The party secretary had been a member of the Red Army, and was not educated, but he had a long revolutionary history, so he wasn't afraid of any authority. He could do what he wanted to do, and he wasn't afraid to accept me, even though it was a crime to accept me. Everyone there knew it was considered a crime, but he didn't care. If a person is good in "Siberia," no one cares.

Alice sits quietly for a while, then gets up and shows me her small garden and says, "I've been farming over the weekend. The compost from my bin in the backyard was just like earth! I'd put skin from fruit, everything, and when I turned it I could see only earth, so I put it over my vegetables here."

She gives me some of her greens to take home saying, "I don't know what you call these in English. Just chop them up and put a lot of salt on them, and just let them sit. No, not in the refrigerator. I add them to tofu, but you can add to chicken or pork as well."

I take the greens home, follow her instructions and add them to my weekly batch of chicken soup. Even my husband agrees they add a nice flavor for a change.

8. "Siberia"

萝北县第一中学

"Siberia" is a deserted prairie! No hospital or clinic. No place for children. That's why I left my daughter, who was four, with my husband's family in Shanghai, and her younger brother, Otto, in Hangzhou with my mom. I went to "Siberia" pregnant with my third, knowing I would come back for the birth.

My translation was almost finished when I went to join my husband, so I took it with me. He had done some translating too – Asian Indian legends and Hans Christian Andersen fables. We put our manuscripts in a cabinet in the teacher's office in the school there with hopes of someday publishing them. But after the proletarian Cultural Revolution, everything in the cabinet was gone, robbed, all our pages, all our work.

When I first arrived in Lou Bei, the town where we lived, I thought I was just there to suffer. Very difficult to live there. Just survival. Such cold weather, down to forty degrees Celsius below zero. We lived at the middle school. One row of buildings was the classes. One the dining hall. And then the dormitory, where several families lived, each in their own small space.

During the so-called proletarian revolution, "school" was a joke. Each morning we had to assemble in the schoolyard to chant slogans, then we would get orders like "Go to the fields and cut wheat." I got to teach only one sentence in English: "Long live Chairman Mao."

They served food three times a day, but I could hardly eat it -- it was so moldy. Back in Shanghai we ate rice, but in "Siberia" we only had mouldy corn cakes. Difficult to swallow. Bitter. We had no time to cook for ourselves and although we had a store, we couldn't buy anything without food stamps, which we only got once a month: only two and a half ounces of oil, and two ounces of sugar per person. Everything was rationed, even soap. Such control. So we only ate chicken in the winter as something special, and sometimes we could buy pork, but only two ounces a month. In the summer there was an outdoor market so we could get more vegetables.

The Amur river was less than an hour away from Lou Bei, but we didn't have any fish to eat. The Chinese call the Amur river "The Black Dragon." I heard that the fishermen there would sit on top of the ice and use a steel stick with a sharp point to chop a hole and the fish would jump out of the hole. But they would keep most of the fish for themselves. We never saw any in our town.

After a few months I went back to Hangzhou for the birth of our third child, a boy. I still wanted to work, not stay at home and be a housewife. So I weaned the baby on rice soup and goat's milk and left him with his older brother and my mom in Hangzhou.

After I got back, I cashed in my investment in government bonds and bought a sewing machine. You had to use your feet to run it. No, not a Singer, but the famous Chinese brand: Butterfly. I learned to sew everything: my husband's shirts, my children's clothes. Whenever we went back to Shanghai, people thought I had a new suit. We didn't want our family to know we were poor, so we pretended to be rich. Actually, I made all my clothes by turning my husband's old clothes to the other side, and I made the clothes for my children from my old clothes and sent them in packages back to Hangzhou and Shanghai. Material was very expensive. Only my husband got new suits, and we bought the children one new suit each for Chinese New Year when we were back in Shanghai.

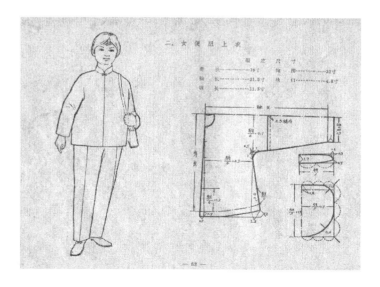

We sent money to my mother for the boys, but my father-in-law – who outlived my husband, worked until he was ninety, and lived to almost a hundred years – he told us to save our money for trips back to see the children, which we managed to do every year during winter vacation. Summer vacation was too short, only two weeks, and it took a week to travel each direction. So we went in the winter when we had more than a month, sometimes two months. We would start by ox and cart from our house in the country, then by bus, then by train, and then by ship from the port Dalian to Shanghai.

I wonder what it would be like to leave your children and see them only once a year, but I don't ask. I don't want to sound judgemental or force my Western values upon her story. In China, it seems, you do what's expedient – the most important thing is to work for your country. At that time in Communist China they couldn't afford to indulge themselves with their children. Besides, leaving them with the grandparents seemed better for the children than taking them to "Siberia."

I try to keep focused on what Alice is saying, and the next statement surprises me as well.

During this time, my husband and I had a good life in "Siberia." We taught together in a middle school, and helped each other, and improved the school so that our teaching group became a model for the whole province. Since I had no children with me, and we left them with our parents, the only thing I thought about at that time was teaching. So I developed a special relationship with my students. I liked my students and they liked me very much. They were so good at Russian, and could write such articles! We put them up on a wall journal, with some students having three or four pages on display. I'm still in touch with many of my students and proud of what they have achieved.

After three years of living in the school's dormitory, we were assigned to a small hut, and our life got even better. We said good-bye to the dining hall and I started trying to cook a little. The families of our students gave us rice because they knew it was what we wanted most of all. The hut had thick, solid walls made from earth and straw, especially thick at the bottom to keep out the cold. Every year when winter came we had to add a layer to the walls.

When I start asking questions about her house, Alice draws out a floor plan for me on a scrap piece of paper.

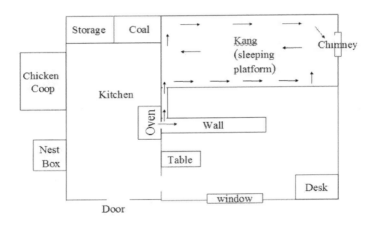

We had a one room with a kang, a raised platform where we could sleep. Under the kang the smoke and heat from the coal fire wound its way through ducts and kept us warm, and then went out the chimney. At first our fire was in the main room, but later we added a kitchen, and the coal fire heated a small, hollow wall in the main room and then went under the kang. We had a desk for writing and I covered my sewing machine with a board for meals.

In the winter every government worker got money for compensation to buy coal. A truck can carry four tons of coal and at first they gave us two tons for the winter, but as the government got poorer, only one ton. We used the coal for heat, but straw and wood under a large iron pot for cooking.

We kept cabbage, carrots, and potatoes underground in the winter so they would stay fresh for several months. We had our own garden in the front and more space in the back to plant vegetables and beans. We could buy seeds in town, or get them from our neighbors. In the winter I would grow bean sprouts on the windowsill in the kitchen.

For a while we had a good life.

9. Cultural Revolution

文化大革命

In 1966 the proletarian Cultural Revolution changed our lives dramatically. They shut down all the schools. Learning is not important, Mao Zedong taught, only working. No classes. All the time: meetings, meetings, struggle, criticize someone. Teachers were divided into two political groups. One said: Long live the Communist Party. The other said: The current party is counter-revolutionary, not the real Communist Party.

This time I just stepped aside. Nothing to do with me, I said. I became a family woman. Just did housework. I asked my neighbors to teach me how to cook better. I sat and watched the local tailor – watching is learning – and my sewing improved. I bought a book that taught me how to make patterns.

By this time we knew how to control. But my sister, who was rich because her husband worked as an engineer, who at forty years old, needed nothing –

just a child. No one is as close to me as this sister. Giving a child to a childless family member was a common practice in China at that time. She could have asked her husband's sister, but she chose me and my husband.

However, I had trouble with this pregnancy. In the eighth month, I fainted and found out I had low blood pressure. We had no telephones, so we telegraphed my mom, and she came up north to be with me. She took care of me, prayed for me, and I got well enough that she said I could make the trip back to Shanghai to have the baby. But I went into labor on the way back as we were approaching the city of Nanjing. There would be a long delay to cross the width of the lower Yangtze, one train car at a time on a ship, so they let me get off at the station just before Nanjing and pushed me in a cart to a nearby hospital. There our fourth child, a boy, was born. I stayed two days, then we got back on the train, went on to Shanghai, and gave the baby to my sister.

Alice, in the traditional Chinese manner, is very stoical about her life. Working seems the supreme value and children are often passed on to the extended family. I keep trying not to interject my Western values on her, but I agonize about her being separated from her children. And at this point I can no longer stand it. I want to know about her relationship with the son she gave to her sister.

"Yes, I think he knows I am his mother, but we never speak of it. I think maybe a neighbor told him."
This is all she has to say. I don't pry for more.
She moves on to a new event.

In 1969 during the proletarian cultural revolution, students were supposed to "keep moving" – travel all over China by train to get to know different places, staying in schools. They would travel without invitation, just go wherever they wanted – no restrictions, no control. They packed into the trains. No passes, no tickets. Just push and shove your way in.

They could come into your homes, search anything, take anything they wanted. They went to my mom's house in Hangzhou. They made her and my family go to the gate and wait, while in her yard they dug three feet under the loose floor boards looking for an arsenal of guns they thought might be there since my father had been in the Kuomintang army. Yes, crazy. They ransacked my mom's jewellery. They broke a solid jade bracelet into two pieces. I later glued it back for her. My son has it now in Hangzhou.

During this time we had nothing to do, nothing to do but travel, so my husband decided to go to Shanghai. I was afraid to go with him. But after he left, a woman, the secretary of the youth league, wanted to go to travelling, and asked me if I would go with her. I thought I would be politically safe with her and I wanted to see my children so I said, of course. When we got to the station we found it so crowded, I thought I wasn't going to get on. She was bigger than me and pushed her way onto the train, but I couldn't get through the crowd. I was so eager to go home and see my children, I started screaming and crying out, and some people lifted me up and passed me through the train window!

That period ended, and they swung to the other extreme. They clamped down on travel and we had to return to Lou Bei. I went back with the youth secretary and the criticism had just about run down. They could not find any more enemies, so they found me, an historic enemy. They said: Let's criticize the old one, the counter-revolutionary. Then came my turn. In the town square, they posted my name saying I was an old member of the right wing. This time it didn't bother me so much, and they didn't criticize my husband at all. He had joined the conservative group, wrote and printed a respected newsletter.

By 1972 we had been up north for ten years. I was forty years old and we decided we wanted very much to have another child – one we could keep. By then we had a hospital I could go to. A lot easier to live in "Siberia" than before, so it's okay to have another child. We thought we wouldn't ever get back to Shanghai to be with our other children, because of the strict system for moving. You cannot move anywhere you like. Too many papers, local administrators, etcetera. So I got pregnant again with my fifth child.

One morning Alice agrees to go to Tai Chi with me at our local community center. She stops by on her bike and I follow her on mine. When a car pulls out in front of her on our street, she makes a U-turn in an intersection and circles back. We turn left at the railroad tracks, then right across the tracks and down a busy street. Where I usually get off my bike and use the pedestrian crossing she suddenly juts out her left arm and shoots across. I walk across and catch up with her at the bike rack outside the center.

The class is already in session when we go inside. I stand in the front row and she finds a space at the back. I can see her in the mirror and notice she keeps up, follows, even anticipates the instructor. When we do Tai Chi together by the lagoon, we only do about half an hour. As the class approaches and even runs over an hour, I can tell Alice's legs are tired. She says afterwards, yes, "too long." And "I couldn't hear what she was saying."

We sit outside the senior activity room where they serve lunches, and Alice tells me she once played the piano there in the dining hall.

A woman passes by us, and says hello to Alice.

"Did Alice tell you what a good ping-pong player she is? She's a terrific athlete. And she plays the piano. She's played beautifully for us here in the lunchroom."

Alice laughs in her self-effacing way. The woman moves inside for her lunch, and Alice tells me a little more of her story.

Just after the birth of our last child, a son, another big change in our lives happened. At the end of the Cultural Revolution, schooling started again, but they said, "We don't need any foreign languages." So they kicked us out of the teaching staff, and sent us to work on a collective farm in the country.

The farmers didn't see us as enemies. They loved us and gave us everything we needed, just like the Communist Party once had done. They sent us straw for our fires. When winter was coming they sent us a whole cart of coal, also cabbage and carrots which we stored underground like we did before in Lou Bei. Our home was one room with a kang, and a kitchen we shared with another family in a room on the other side.

My husband managed a dining hall for the young people that had also been moved to the country to work on the farm. He had to get up very early each morning. Since I had a one-month old baby, they let me stay at home to control a small locked cabinet, a sort of sub-station bank, for deposit and withdrawal of small amounts of money. If I got too much money, I would have to go to the bank in town. How did I get there? On a tractor!

We had stayed on the farm for three years, when they wanted us to teach again. When it comes to teaching foreign languages, China is like a pendulum. When it leans to the left, no foreign languages. When it moves back to the right, they want us to teach foreign languages. Now they wanted us to come back to Lou Bei and teach again. But since China's relationship with Russia had broken down, they no longer wanted us to teach Russian. This time we were supposed to teach English.

They built new houses for us, a little bit bigger, with a separate kitchen, but they were basically built on the same design. We had a bigger yard so I started raising a dozen or so chickens. Using my carpenter skills, I built a chicken coop against the kitchen wall where they could keep warm from the heater, and made a separate place for them to nest and lay their eggs. We'd get four or five, at least three a day. We'd share these with friends and they would share things with us. In the spring I would let one of the hens sit on her eggs for hatching. I'd get maybe twenty chicks and I would give some of them to neighbor friends. I would keep maybe ten of them and in the winter we would kill all but five or six hens that I would keep in the kitchen in a cage. I would put a wooden branch in the cage for them to stand on, and under it put ash from the cooking for padding to catch the eggs and the poo poo, then clean it out every day.

10. Back to Hangzhou

回故乡

In 1976, after I had been teaching English again for three years, my mother had a stroke. When I got back to Hangzhou, she could still talk, and walked with a cane. I hired a nanny for her, but no one could stand working for her because of her bad temper. When I talked to my mom, she would say bad things about my sister and her husband. It seems I'm the only person she doesn't have a temper with, so I asked for permission to move back to Hangzhou permanently. Before I left I spent a year training my replacement to teach English. We moved back to Hangzhou when my youngest was six.

My mom and I got along fine, but I missed my husband. I was allowed to teach languages in a Hangzhou middle school, but I didn't like it because at that time they divided all the good students into one class, and the worse students in another. They gave me the worst students. They behaved terribly -- very

79

disruptive, talking all the time. You see, the Gang of Four, which included Mao Zedong's wife and my husband's classmate, Yao Wen Yang, taught that learning a foreign language was of no use and its teachers were not to be respected.

At last the Gang of Four had been smashed and now was a different time. I couldn't teach in such an atmosphere until I finally thought of ways to discipline them and they started to slowly get better. How did I do that? First things first. I needed to make them interested in learning a foreign language, to motivate them. What's the use of a foreign language? I told them this:

"You are living in a new time, the end of the twentieth century. Now China has more relations with other countries than before. You will be the masters of the future time. Don't look down upon yourselves. You must have an aim in life. More and more foreigners are coming to China, and our West Lake is such a famous, scenic spot, and we have famous historical buildings in memory of our Chinese heroes.

You will have many opportunities to talk with the people who come to see them."

Things were opening up. I could talk to my former classmates again. I found out that Mr. Chen, my former classmate, had become a teacher in a middle school in Shanghai. His wife, my good friend named Snowy, worked in a quilt shop. Someone gave me her address so I went to see her.

What a reunion we had! It had been over twenty years since we'd last seen each other. We rejoiced in the fact that the Gang of Four had been smashed, the Cultural Revolution was over and we could be friends again. I told her about my life in "Siberia" and she told me about hers in Shanghai.

The government had asked Snowy to be a teacher also, but she said "I won't be an intellectual. I will live like a worker." At that time clever people were called smelly, stinky intellectuals and she didn't want to be called that. So she worked in a quilt shop, making feather quilts and selling them. Beautiful quilts. She gave me one, which I still keep with my daughter in Shanghai.

I went back to see Snowy many times, sometimes for dinner at her apartment with her husband, who after a while got a job as an editor of an encyclopedia. The last time I saw her, she told me that she had breast cancer and wasn't expected to live. She gave me her photo.

She died in 1980, and Mr. Chen came to the USA but he disappeared. We lost contact with him. No one knew where he was, not even his mother. When I came here I couldn't find him. I heard that his sisters worked for the United Nations, but I didn't know their names.

After a year of being apart, my husband had trained a replacement for himself in "Siberia" so he was allowed to come back to Hangzhou. He got a job teaching English at the electricity bureau, then got a position at the bureau's institute, a training center, for electrical power companies. The institute was located in the north part of Hangzhou, and it took him an hour or more to get there, so they gave us an apartment nearby. Because my husband was so well-liked, he was able to get me an appointment to teach at the institute as well with a small salary, just enough for food. My mom moved with us. So our family was together again, and we got to see the older children more often. Our daughter was nearby in Shanghai and our two sons at the university.

二十世纪八十年代初于杭州BF乙笑相
搭乃林

We lived on the third floor of the apartment building, so my mom couldn't get down to the ground floor or get outside by herself. "I'm in jail!" she kept saying. Since my teaching place was so close, I could check on her between classes. Only on holidays could we help her down to go outside. She wasn't happy.

Friends from her church would come visit her, but that's the only activity she had.

She lived with us several more years. Then she had a fall. We got her to bed and she seemed okay, but a couple of days later when we came back from the school, she had died.

Life went on without her. Our students at the new institute were very bright, students of high quality, and we had great success with them. My husband stayed with one class that he had started, and I started with a new class. We only had them four or five hours a week for three semesters compared to students at senior middle school who were going on to a university that had three full years of a foreign language. After three years of senior middle school at this institute our students would be sent to America or Germany to take training in electrical engineering at power companies there. So English as a foreign language was very important for them, even though to them the textbooks about electricity were more important. So before they took their exams, we devised a short course to brush up on their English. They did as well on the exams as the university students who had ten years of English. They hadn't fallen behind, but just the opposite, so the advanced authorities at the institute liked us very much.

I started to play ping-pong again with my co-workers at the institute, just as I had in Dalian at the Russian Institute. We also played Chinese checkers and chess. But we had no competitions, no clubs of any kind. They invited someone to teach us Tai Chi, so I learned eight beginning forms, but I didn't really have enough time to practice. Even outside of class time, in the morning and the evenings, I was helping students. Later when I was retired, I saw them doing Tai Chi in the park, so I joined them every morning. That is where I learned from a master. My husband went with me, and we learned it together, but he didn't take it as seriously as I did.

I taught at the institute in Hangzhou from 1980-1986. In 1987, when I was only fifty-five years old, I found out I had to retire – a requirement for all women of that age in China. I was so angry. The job still needed me. There was no one to take my place, and my husband didn't have to retire until he was sixty. Now he had to do all the teaching, plus administrative work as well. So I helped him. If I didn't work my husband would be too tired.

Since I had worked for more than thirty-five years, I retired at full salary. Two years later, they got a new teacher, so I thought: Now I'll just stay at home. But at that time there were not enough qualified English teachers in Hangzhou, so a classmate from Dalia Institute who was teaching at a local industrial university got me a job there. They paid me much more than I was earning before, and I got that on top of my retirement salary. They also had a school bus I could take there.

In a change of policy, just to make a show, the party decided to invite some intellectuals to become members. They asked my husband, and he couldn't refuse. The Tiananmen Square protests began in the spring 1989 and by mid-May had spread to hundreds of other cities. We had such sympathy for the student protests and my husband had to tell the secretary of the party what he thought about everything, so he got criticized for this. But since he had such a good relationship with the leaders, they didn't criticize him much. I was retired and not a party member, so they left me alone.

11. Two Countries

两个国家

There's a chilly wind blowing, so we meet inside Alice's apartment with a cup of tea as Alice continues her story.

When my husband retired in 1993 the institute gave us another apartment in town. Shortly before that time my son Otto had immigrated to USA. He went for one year, and then his wife went and I kept my granddaughter who was going to kindergarten with me. Then they decided everything was okay and they wanted me to bring them their daughter. So my husband and I decided to go to USA and stay a while to earn some US dollars and take them back to China. No problem getting a passport. So we went abroad, leaving our last son to stay in our apartment.

I liked life in the USA. I enjoyed the relations between people. I was impressed right away. For example, when I went with my granddaughter to the school, the teachers were so warm. They came to us and explained what we have to do. They even let us go to an English class for adults and gave us a small booklet introducing the school and the local culture. I wrote in my dairy: Mao Zedong always told us to serve the people, but during Mao Zedong's own time everyone in the government, even small departments, was so proud – not helpful at all. When you went to them for something they would say, go there, and when you go to that place they sent you back. They don't want to talk to you, they don't want to work, they don't want to serve anyone. They'd just sit reading a novel. But here, in the USA, they serve the people in reality. They make things so easy for us. Such a bright contrast.

My husband lived with our son Otto in Fremont, but I lived nearby in a big house with a family and took care of children for a lady from Taiwan, a very special lady. I liked her very much and she liked me. Her husband owned a company that made integrated circuits and he was looking for some help in the factory, so I recommended my husband. We got green cards, and ended up staying for a little over a year. He learned how to drive our son's car, even on the highway. I wanted to drive too, but Otto said he wouldn't teach me. "No," he said, "One is enough!"

When we went back to China we thought at last we would be rich. But at the bank, everyone else was already rich too! I saw them with big stacks of money!

We had the chance to buy an apartment at a very low price, so we did. We thought we would do nothing now, just enjoy our life. My son stayed with us a while until he married. I bought a piano at a shop in Hangzhou and I thought I could just sit at home and play.

First show of tulips in Prince Bay Park , 1995

Once again, the situation changed. One day some people came to our house in a car saying they need a Russian interpreter for a local factory that made clothes. Actually, what happened, the Russians gave us an airplane, and in exchange for that we were to make clothes for them to sell in Russian. So they sent their clothes designer from Russia. First I said, No, I can't do that. I haven't done much with Russian for forty years! But they said, Oh, nobody else can

91

understand. Please help us. We have a car outside waiting. Please, let's go. Okay, I said, Let me try. So I went with them. It turned out the Russian designer had an English interpreter he would speak to in English, and then the interpreter would translate to Chinese.

So, yes, a lot was getting lost in the translations. When they talked to each other in Russian, I understood, and when they talked to each other in English, I understood. I thought: I can do this! My Russian came back just listening and I helped out a little that day. Then they came again and again for me in their car, until finally I became permanent. They paid me a little, but more than my retirement salary.

Later my husband came to the factory to help out too. He would travel with the Soviet clothes designer to buy material, fabric and small decorations, trimmings. They made sports clothes, like ski jackets. And we employees could sometimes buy them.

At this point Alice jumps up, "I still have one. I'll show you." runs into her bedroom and brings out a black, red, and gray all-weather jacket, very Western looking, like a ski jacket, with the English words: Jr. SELA Club on one of the pockets. "This is a coat I bought for my grandson, but when he outgrew it, I added the cuffs, so I can wear."

My recorder has run out of batteries. Alice takes some out of her desk, and while my recorder is recharging she says, "I have something to tell you. I'm moving to Sunnyvale. But I will come back to visit."

While I worry about will we really have enough time to finish working on the book together she goes on. "I'm lonely here. In Sunnyvale I have lots of Chinese friends. And the Chinese church. Now Otto is very busy, and it takes him an hour to drive over here. So, I will miss my beautiful place to live here, but I need to be with my friends and family."

We have two weeks before she goes, so we vow to spend as much time as possible working together.

About this time, when I'm feeling under pressure to finish Alice's story before she moves, I meet another woman from Shanghai. In fact, she's the new landlady of a duplex across the street from me. Young enough to be Alice's daughter, she is a very assertive businesswoman. When I tell her about Alice, she says she wants to meet her. I'm on my way to meet with Alice and suggest she join us later. I tell Alice before we begin our session that we might

have a visitor, and we go ahead and start, I secretly hoping the woman wouldn't show up. I imagine them going on and on in Mandarin, and me left there sitting with an unfinished story.

Alice no sooner starts a critical part of her story, when I see the new woman from Shanghai coming down the street. "Oh dear, here she comes," I mutter.

Alice jumps up and hurries over to greet her. And back they come, speaking as I feared in Mandarin. But once they sit down with me, they make the effort to speak in English, and I am touched by that. Still, after a while, I butt in.

"We're just getting to an important part of the story . . . when her husband gets ill." Alice looks at me, nods, and looks to her new friend, who also nods. "I'll just listen," she says, "if that's all right." This time I nod and turn on the recorder.

We had only been back from the U.S. for three years, and he was only sixty-six. Too young to die. Such a shock. He was always so healthy – never went to a doctor. He didn't know he was sick. He was still travelling with the clothes designer. And then we discovered he had cancer. It happened very fast, less than four months.

One night he felt some pain inside. I was always feeling pain, here, there, everywhere, but he seldom felt pain. I had a heating pad, and at midnight he got up and took that heating pad. I said, "What's the matter with you? If you have such pain, you have to go to the doctor."

Early in the morning I went to register him for an appointment. On that day they gave him a scan, and then radiation and put him in the hospital. That was at the beginning of the New Year. I lived in the hospital with him, they asked me to stay because there were not enough nurses. At night I slept on a reclining chair. It was a hospital of Western medicine, but he had a lot of pain, so I got some Chinese medicine for him and they allowed me to put some on his spine, and then he didn't get so much pain. He wanted surgery. It was too late the doctor said, it wouldn't make a difference. But my husband insisted. He just wanted it out, so they did the surgery. It was too spread to remove it. He died shortly later.

During this time I started praying to God. My mother's Christian friends came to visit and prayed with me. My husband prayed with me too. When he died, I just believed I had to get some punishment from God.

When she says this, I feel my heart go thud. Our new friend protests, "What? Why did you believe that?"

Now I'm glad she's there with us.

"Because I didn't believe in God for thirty years. Since the time I started to believe in Communism."

"Do you still believe that?" I ask.

"Yes. I think that God gives me punishment. I wrote bad things about God in my self-criticism. My mother's friends didn't think that. Just I thought that."

I can no longer keep silent and say, " I just hope that when you go back to the church in Sunnyvale that you will talk to the pastor there, and that you will think about the God you believe in. Does God punish, or does God love you?"

"Through the punishment, God gave me love. Otherwise, I couldn't come back to God. God

controls everything. God is all-powerful. The church is not God. And one pastor is different from another. So I just believe in God. Otherwise you cannot get a right explanation. God controls nature, and the universe. In the end, even Karl Marx believed in God."

With that she continues with her story.

After my husband died, I thought I couldn't live. I didn't know where to go or what to do. I was like a kite flying in the wind whose string has broken.

My daughter helped me a lot after my husband died, and took me into her home in Shanghai. She got me going again. A shopping mall in a huge building in Shanghai was holding a "United Nations" second language competition. My daughter encouraged me to enter it. I said it had been too many years, forty years, since I'd done written Russian, but she said I had to try.

So I went and took the written test. I thought I did terrible, so I just turned it in and came home. But after I got home, the phone rang, and they gave me the oral test over the phone. I won! I got a big prize of money to spend at the mall, so I bought lots of things for my daughter's home.

A year later I started travelling with some of my classmates from the Russian Institute. We went all over Europe. Finally, in 2005, I decided to come to the USA. This time to stay.

At first I lived with Otto in San Jose. I went to worship at the Methodist Church. I taught English as a Second Language at that church for a year to the older Chinese ladies and gentlemen. I would type up the English lesson on my son's computer, send it to the church and they would print it. I'm not good at conversation but I am good at grammar. Especially for adults, grammar helps a lot. Usually I'm not patient. But for teaching I always have patience. Yes, teaching is learning.

These students became my friends, very good friends. Sometimes I didn't even live with my son, I lived at my friends. Actually, in the USA all Chinese are good friends because we understand each other and we don't have to explain the political situation. We speak in Mandrian. Most Cantonese understand Mandrian, but I cannot speak Cantonese.

After two years I got my own place in Santa Cruz. I still go back to San Jose to see my family and friends there, like at Chinese New Years. We get together for several days and everyone brings a dish and we eat and talk. But since we are Christian, no special ceremonies. That is mostly for the Buddhists. I go to worship at the Methodist Church. And I see my friends there.

I thank Alice for her time, and leave the two women to carry on their conversation, hoping after talking more to her, Alice will take on board what we have said.

Sure enough, the next time I meet Alice she says straight away, "I thought about what you said last time. You are right. God didn't punish me. I brought the punishment on myself."

That wasn't quite what I had hoped for, but certainly closer.

12. A Tribute to Alice

赞爱丽斯

In our last session, Alice returns to her favorite subject: her success with her students. I think this is what she'd most like to be remembered for. But to me, she is so much more.

In 2008 I went back up north in China to Luo Bei, and I was greeted so warmly. After all, I ended up teaching Russian for 20 years in the middle school there. I still keep in touch with many of my students. Many of them are now retired and some of them are quite rich.

In 2011 I went back to China for my 79th birthday, which the Chinese celebrate instead of the 80th. More than ten students came down from Luo Bei to Hangzhou.

After just two years of learning Russian (the old matelanguage I taught them) some of those students could write an article in Russian of more than 500 words. The worst student could not pronounce words clearly because his tongue is too big. But still he chose Russian as his speciality, and later he worked in the army. There was some event in 1980 with fighting between the Russian and Chinese, and he went there to cry out for peace to the Soviet soldiers and convinced them to stop fighting.

Impatient with this conversation, I have something else in mind. A few days earlier, Alice's "caregiver" (she calls by his last name, Shaw) brought us something he had written about Alice and gives me permission to use it. I ask Alice if we can now go over it. You can see from the different color inks, and different slants of the pen, that he wrote this over a period of time, but it's all scrunched up in one big block that makes it so hard to read that Alice wants me to read it to her. I ask her if I can run the recorder while I'm reading.

These are the words Shaw wrote:

The Little Teacher

When I just moved into my new apartment, a presentation in the community room had just finished. As we were leaving a tiny Chinese lady said to me, "I don't understand all. You help translate, please?"

"Sure," I smiled as she was so cute, and earnest in her asking. I was delighted with her straight away. We went to her apartment, where I crossed out a lot of words and highlighted the important stuff.

"Oh, thank you. You make it simple, clear."

"No problem, any time you need translation, I'll be glad to help you." Her eyes lit up and with a big smile put her hands together and bowed several times like a little doll.

Alice laughs when she hears me read this.

She told me her Chinese name, which I still can't pronounce, but thank God she said, "My American name is Alice. Do you like the name Alice? Why did I choose that name? Because Beethoven wrote beautiful music, dedicated to Elise." She put both hands to her heart and smiled huge. "His music is wonderful."

"I think he needs a good drummer, myself, a rhythm section. I'm more into jazz."

"Oh, I like Stephen Foster as well: Old Man River, Old Black Joe."

"I thought you were from China. Where'd you learn Stephen Foster and Beethoven?"

"Why, in a Christian refugee camp. I learned to play the piano there."

"You have a story, huh?"

"I have stories," she answered. "But I must eat now, we'll talk later, okay?" she bowed several times. So I said good-bye and left her there bobbing.

Bobbing? Alice asks me. Yes, bobbing up and down, I demonstrate. She chuckles.

From then on, if I saw her working in her garden I would go over and talk with her and she was always extremely pleasant, positive, and had a wonderful outlook on life. I never knew anyone so delighted in the smallest things. She was charming and just thinking about her made me laugh. One day she asked me what I do with all my free time now that I am retired. "Well, I used to paint and write stories, but I'm not inspired for years to do either. I play tennis on the week-ends .

My friends moved away or are so busy scrambling to survive in these times, they have no time to be social anymore. So the answer is: Not much. How 'bout you? What do you do?"

"Same. My husband passed away ten years ago. All my children are grown and live in China, except one son. He has a young family and doesn't have time for me, so I too am alone. I play piano, watch TV, and play solitaire on the computer," she shrugged. "I talk with my family in China by Skype on the week-ends."

"How long have you been here in the USA, and why did you leave China?"

"China is too hot, and too cold in the winter, and never sunshine because of so much industry. You get a lot of bad coughs there. My son got a job in San Jose in computers. I lived with him and his wife for a period of time but I once came to Santa Cruz to visit an old school mate. I liked the fresh air from the sea, sunny and cool, perfect for me."

The next day I was at wits end what to do so I called little Alice, "What ya doing?"

She laughed. "Nothing. What are you doing?"

"Nothing," I answered, "Want to do nothing together?" That really made her laugh. She has a big laugh for such a little thing.

Indeed, Alice is laughing as I read this.

"You have bike? Let's ride on West Cliff Drive. I'll follow you," she said. So we hopped on bikes and headed for West Cliff.

In the old promenade tradition, with a modern, sporty twist, West Cliff Drive is where people in Santa Cruz go to walk, jog, ride bikes, see and be seen.

We stopped to rest and watched the surfers several times. She was all smiles. We crossed the street, and entered on a dirt path in Lighthouse Fields, which is wild and where people exercise their dogs. The paths go everywhere and I can hear her behind me shouting, "Oh how wonderful." We came to stop at a huge, fallen tree. I sat down and she laid down to get some sun. Then out of her backpack she produced some snacks she brought from China, also two small cups, and a thermos of green tea.

Alice is laughing again.

How sweet, I thought.

And that was the first cup of endless green tea she served to me. I started going over to her place, only a few doors away from my place. I referred to it as Little Alice's Tea Hut.

Alice laughs with delight.

Tea was the first thing every time. One evening she asks, "Do you play Chinese checkers?"

"When I was a kid,"

"Want to play now?" Turns out it's very different from the way I was taught as a child. I loved it and from then on I played Chinese Checkers and had tea every evening, which I'll always remember as some of the sweetest times of my life. And if I didn't finish the little pot of tea, five or ten minutes after returning to my apartment I would hear a tap on my window, look out, and there would be little Alice with a big smile holding the pot.

Alice laughs.

When I first met her she was studying to pass tests as an American citizen. So we would stop at a bench in the sun and I would quiz her. Although she always knew the answers, she was concerned about passing the test. When she took the test she did not miss one question and became a USA citizen.

We often laughed over the misunderstanding of an English word. Once we were walking to the wharf when she asked me, "What does that sign mean -- a complete auto body shop?" So I told her they fix the bodies of cars. She burst out laughing "I thought maybe not such a good place - they bend bodies of us!" And being a language teacher, she wants always to be corrected if she mispronounces something.

Alice taught many Chinese people just "off the boat" the English she knows and always for free. She is humble and always considerate, compassionate, and helpful, and on and on and on. She is one of the finest people I have ever known.

At this ending Alice laughs on and on, in waves of doubt, delight, and gratitude.

"He says when I move, I have to come see him once a week, and he'll come see me once a week, so we can see each other twice a week. He suggested this but I think it's too difficult to do that, because a lot of things happen after moving."

But at this printing Shaw is still visiting her once a week in Sunnyvale.

Before I leave what I thought might be my last session with her, I ask Alice if she will play Beethoven's *Fur Elise* for me and let me record it. "Come back tomorrow," she says. "I must practice."

Her piano is an old upright, decorated with Christmas tinsel even though it's July. She begins playing with an intense, serious face and great precision. If she makes a mistake she exclaims and goes back to correct it. But the melody comes out loud and strong, and when she ends it, she breaks into a self-depreciating laugh.

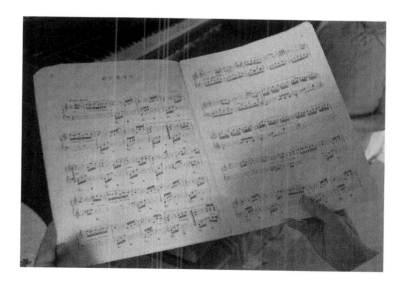

Dana Bagshaw is a playwright and author. Two of her plays, *Cell Talk* and *Hilda, Daughter of Woden*, take place in medieval England and have been published in the UK. Two novels, *Mama Grace* and *Running From Grace*, based on manuscripts from her pioneering family in Oklahoma, have been published in the US. She is currently working on a third book, *Facing Grace,* and a new play about African asylum seekers.